Sheila M. Nelson

RIGHT FROM THE START

Twenty Tunes

for Young Violinists

Piano Part

Boosey & Hawkes
Music Publishers Limited
London · New York · Bonn · Sydney · Tokyo

COMPOSER'S NOTE

The pieces in this book were designed to help young beginners to overcome the problems of music reading by taking very small steps, so giving them time to get things **'Right from the Start'**. The availability of a disc can greatly stimulate practice in the early days, and will encourage the student to sing the tunes before playing them — a necessary stage in the process of learning to play in tune.

Many of the early pieces are particularly suited to bowing variations, and suitable rhythm patterns are indicated at the end of each piece. 'Ringing Bell' and 'George got out of bed too late' will be the particular favourites for use in this way, allowing bow technique to run well ahead of fingering, so that the sounds produced are as pleasant as possible. Rhythm patterns may be learned with the aid of the words provided.

The finger-charts and easy melodies using only four notes on one string to be found in **Tetratunes**, provide useful supplementary material to this volume. By the end of it the student will have acquired sufficient technical and reading skills to progress to the pieces in **Stringsongs**, the duets in **Two in One** and the ensemble music in **Together from the Start** and **Tunes for my String Quartet**. All these publications are available from Boosey & Hawkes.

Sheila M. Nelson
London, 1983

ANMERKUNG DER KOMPONISTIN

Die Stücke in diesem Heft sollen jungen Anfängern helfen, sich schon frühzeitig (**'Right from the Start'**, d.h. von Anfang an) in kleinen Lerneinheiten mit den Problemen des Notenlesens auseinanderzusetzen. Die dazu angebotene Schallplatte kann in der ersten Zeit eine wesentliche Hilfe sein und den Schüler dazu anregen, die Melodien zunächst zu singen, bevor er sie spielt — ein notwendiger Schritt innerhalb dieses Lernprozesses.

Viele der kleinen Stücke eignen sich besonders gut für rhythmische Bogenübungen. Entsprechende Variations modelle werden zu Beginn des Heftes vorgestellt und zu jedem Stück ist das dafür geeignete Modell vermerkt. Die Stücke 'Ringing Bell' (deutsch im gleichen Rhythmus sinngemäss: 'Glockenklang') und 'George got out of bed too late' (deutsch im gleichen Rhythmus sinngemäss: 'George kam aus dem Bett zu spät') sind besonders eingängige Übungen, die dem Schüler, noch bevor er mit den Grifftechniken beginnt, ein Gespür für Intonation und Saitenwechsel vermitteln und ihm helfen, schön in diesem Anfangsstadium den Klang so schön wie möglich zu gestalten. Die rhythmischen Modelle können zunächst mit Hilfe von Wortrhythmen geübt werden.

Das **Tetratunes** — Heft mit den dazugehörigen 'finger-charts' (Grifftabellen) und den kleinen Stücken, bei denen nur 4 Töne auf einer Saite zu spielen sind, bietet eine passende Ergänzung. Danach wird der Schüler genügend technische Sicherheit sowie Notenkenntnisse besitzen, um zu **Stringsongs** überzugehen sowie die Duette in **Two in One** und die Ensemblestücke in **Together from the Start** sowie **Tunes for my String Quartet** zu spielen. Sämtliche Ausgaben sind bei Boosey & Hawkes erhältlich.

Sheila M. Nelson
London, 1983

RIGHT FROM THE START

SHEILA M. NELSON

Rhythmic Bowing Variations : to be played by ear

1  *etc.*
Pic-ca-dil-ly Cir - cus   *or*

Pic - ca - dil - ly   Cir - cus

2  *etc.*
Tuppence and threepence and tuppence and

3  *etc.*
Straw - ber-ry rasp-ber-ry   *or*

Straw - ber-ry   rasp - ber-ry

4
Fat-ter than a ca-ter-pil – lar

5  *etc.*
Wa-ter-loo,   Cha-ring Cross   *or*

Wa - ter-loo   Cha-ring Cross

6
Chalk Farm, Cam-den Town

7
Laz – i – ly,   ea – si – ly

8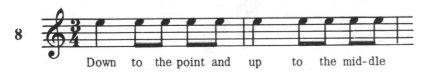
Down to the point and up   to the mid-dle

ACCOMPANIMENTS : for rhythms in 3/4 ; E string

B.& H.20183

4

ACCOMPANIMENTS for rhythms in $\frac{2}{4}$

1　E string

2　A string

3　D string

4　G string

RIGHT FROM THE START

SHEILA M. NELSON

1. ANN, DAN and EGBERT

new material

open E, A, D strings

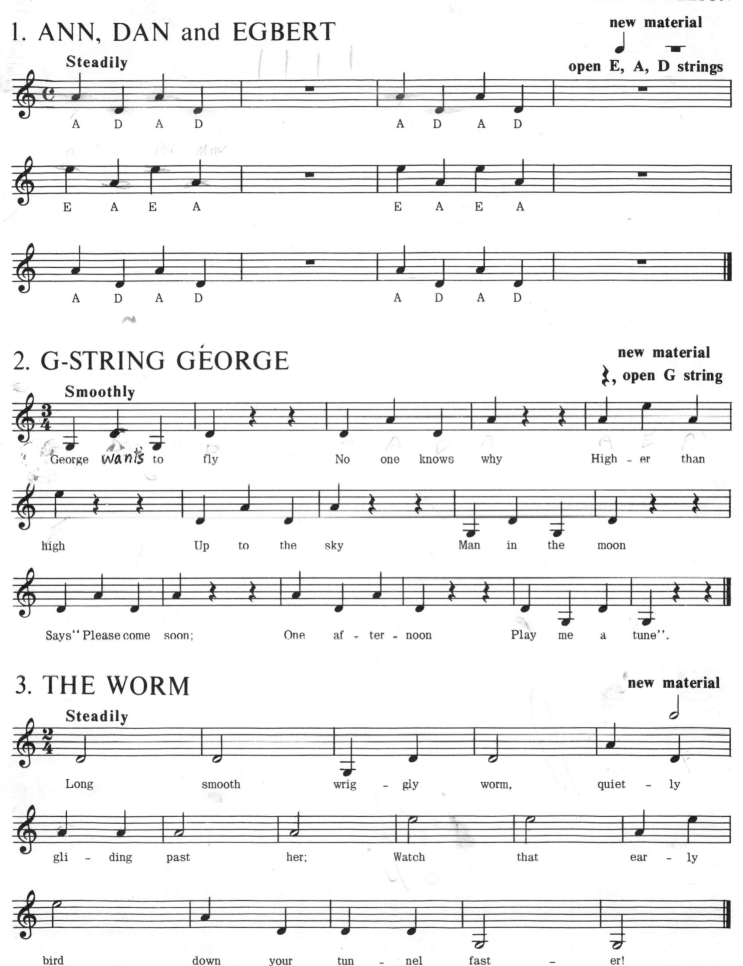

2. G-STRING GEORGE

new material

open G string

George wants to fly   No one knows why   High - er than

high   Up to the sky   Man in the moon

Says " Please come soon;   One af - ter - noon   Play me a tune".

3. THE WORM

new material

Long smooth wrig - gly worm, quiet - ly

gli - ding past her; Watch that ear - ly

bird down your tun - nel fast - er!

2

4. LAZY SONG

5. LATE FOR SCHOOL

6. SWING - BOATS

7. RINGING BELL

8. SAIL IN A PAIL

9. JONATHAN RAT

10. GEORGE GOT OUT OF BED TOO LATE

11. I'VE GOT A FIVEPENCE

4

12. LULLABY

new material
slurs (optional)

Peacefully

Lul - la - by, do not cry, Lul - la, lul - la, lul - la - by.

Snug and warm, free from harm, Safe from dan - ger and a - larm.

Lul - la - by, do not cry, Lul - la, lul - la, lul - la - by.

13. DON'T BOTHER ME

Angrily

"Don't bo -ther me please can't you see I'm just not free now?

Do go a - way, fuss - ing to - day I can - not al - low."

"Yes I can see you're just not free: you're ne - ver free now!

And if I must play with - out fuss, will you tell me how?"

14. RAINY DAY

new material
second finger

Steadily

Dan and Ann went walk - ing, walk - ing, went out walk - ing in the rain;

Tried their boots out in the pud - dles, got ve - ry wet and went home a - gain.

15. THREE IN A BAR

Briskly

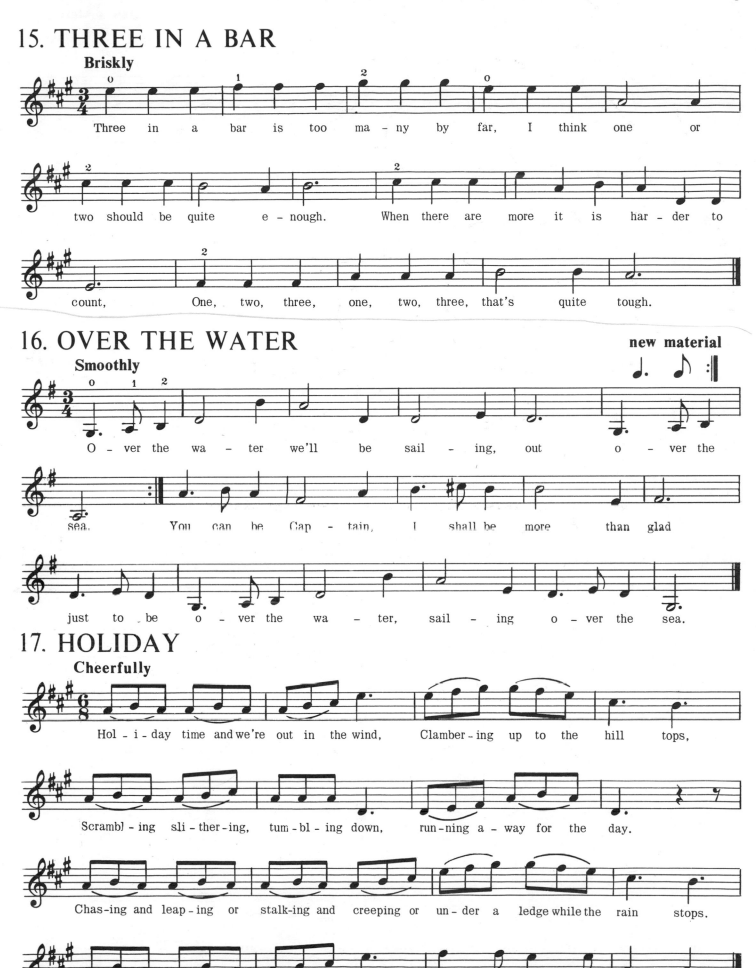

Three in a bar is too ma – ny by far, I think one or two should be quite e – nough. When there are more it is har – der to count, One, two, three, one, two, three, that's quite tough.

16. OVER THE WATER

new material

Smoothly

O – ver the wa – ter we'll be sail – ing, out o – ver the sea. You can be Cap – tain, I shall be more than glad just to be o – ver the wa – ter, sail – ing o – ver the sea.

17. HOLIDAY

Cheerfully

Hol – i – day time and we're out in the wind, Clamber – ing up to the hill tops, Scrambl – ing sli – ther – ing, tum – bl – ing down, run – ning a – way for the day. Chas – ing and leap – ing or stalk – ing and creeping or un – der a ledge while the rain stops. Hol – i – day time is for games in the wind, ne – ver mind the rain – drops.

18. THE CENTIPEDE

new material
♪, third finger

Steadily crawling

19. FIDDLER'S FANCY

new material

Cheerfully

repeat softly

20. COWBOY

new material
fourth finger

Loud and fast

Printed by
Halstan & Co. Ltd., Amersham, Bucks., England

Sheila M. Nelson

RIGHT FROM THE START

Twenty Tunes
for Young Violinists

Violin Part

Boosey & Hawkes
Music Publishers Limited
London · New York · Bonn · Sydney · Tokyo

COMPOSER'S NOTE

The pieces in this book were designed to help young beginners to overcome the problems of music reading by taking very small steps, so giving them time to get things 'Right from the Start'. The availability of a disc can greatly stimulate practice in the early days, and will encourage the student to sing the tunes before playing them — a necessary stage in the process of learning to play in tune.

Many of the early pieces are particularly suited to bowing variations, and suitable rhythm patterns are indicated at the end of each piece. 'Ringing Bell' and 'George got out of bed too late' will be the particular favourites for use in this way, allowing bow technique to run well ahead of fingering, so that the sounds produced are as pleasant as possible. Rhythm patterns may be learned with the aid of the words provided.

The finger-charts and easy melodies using only four notes on one string to be found in **Tetratunes**, provide useful supplementary material to this volume. By the end of it the student will have acquired sufficient technical and reading skills to progress to the pieces in **Stringsongs**, the duets in **Two in One** and the ensemble music in **Together from the Start** and **Tunes for my String Quartet**. All these publications are available from Boosey & Hawkes.

Sheila M. Nelson
London, 1983

ANMERKUNG DER KOMPONISTIN

Die Stücke in diesem Heft sollen jungen Anfängern helfen, sich schon frühzeitig (**'Right from the Start'**, d.h. von Anfang an) in kleinen Lerneinheiten mit den Problemen des Notenlesens auseinanderzusetzen. Die dazu angebotene Schallplatte kann in der ersten Zeit eine wesentliche Hilfe sein und den Schüler dazu anregen, die Melodien zunächst zu singen, bevor er sie spielt — ein notwendiger Schritt innerhalb dieses Lernprozesses.

Viele der kleinen Stücke eignen sich besonders gut für rhythmische Bogenübungen. Entsprechende Variations modelle werden zu Beginn des Heftes vorgestellt und zu jedem Stück ist das dafür geeignete Modell vermerkt. Die Stücke 'Ringing Bell' (deutsch im gleichen Rhythmus sinngemäss: 'Glockenklang') und 'George got out of bed too late' (deutsch im gleichen Rhythmus sinngemäss: 'George kam aus dem Bett zu spät') sind besonders eingängige Übungen, die dem Schüler, noch bevor er mit den Grifftechniken beginnt, ein Gespür für Intonation und Saitenwechsel vermitteln und ihm helfen, schön in diesem Anfangsstadium den Klang so schön wie möglich zu gestalten. Die rhythmischen Modelle können zunächst mit Hilfe von Wortrhythmen geübt werden.

Das Tetratunes — Heft mit den dazugehörigen 'finger-charts' (Grifftabellen) und den kleinen Stücken, bei denen nur 4 Töne auf einer Saite zu spielen sind, bietet eine passende Ergänzung. Danach wird der Schüler genügend technische Sicherheit sowie Notenkenntnisse besitzen, um zu **Stringsongs** überzugehen sowie die Duette in **Two in One** und die Ensemblestücke in **Together from the Start** sowie **Tunes for my String Quartet** zu spielen. Sämtliche Ausgaben sind bei Boosey & Hawkes erhältlich.

Sheila M. Nelson
London, 1983

1. ANN, DAN and EGBERT

new material

open E, A, D strings

Variations : 3 - 6

2. G-STRING GEORGE

new material
{ open G string

Smoothly

mf

George wants to fly   No - one knows why

High - er than high   Up to the sky

Man in the moon   Says "Please come soon;

One af - ter - noon   Play me a tune!"

Variations : 5, 6

B.& H.20183

new material

3. THE WORM

Variation : 3

B.& H.20183

4. LAZY SONG

new material

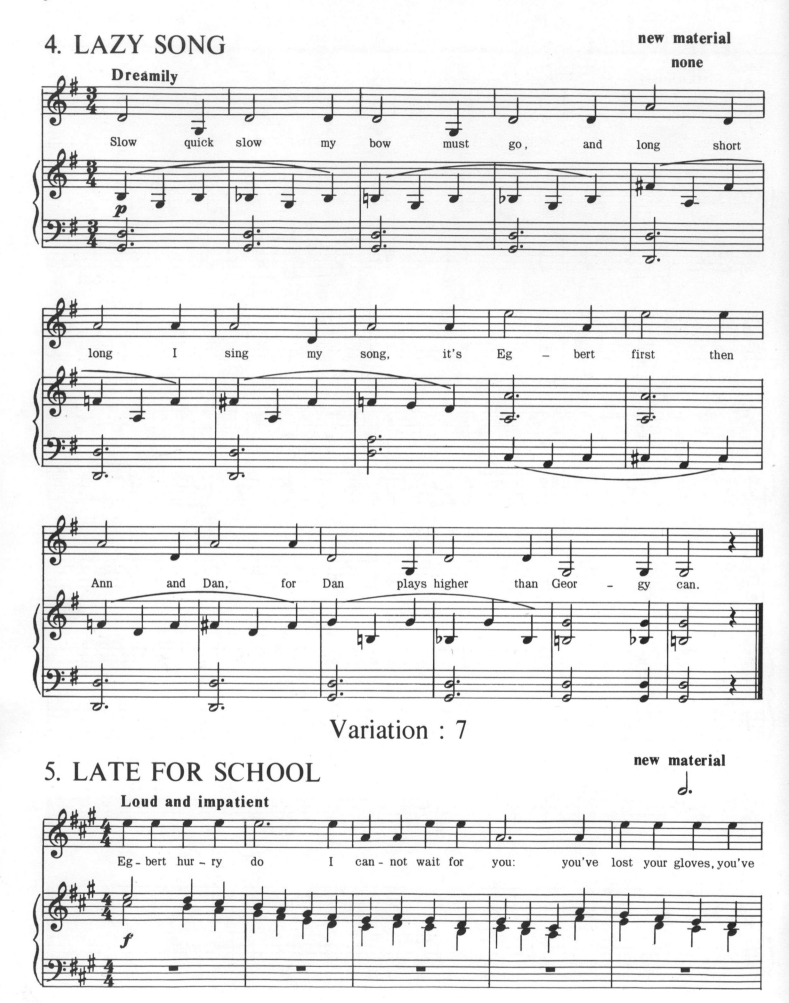

Slow quick slow my bow must go, and long short long I sing my song, it's Eg – bert first then Ann and Dan, for Dan plays higher than Geor – gy can.

Variation : 7

5. LATE FOR SCHOOL

new material

Loud and impatient

Eg – bert hur – ry do I can – not wait for you: you've lost your gloves, you've

Variation : 1

6. SWING-BOATS

new material
none

Quietly rocking

Swing low then swing high, Up and

down and up to the sky, for I can

al – most fly Up to the top and o – ver.

Variations : 7, 8

10

7. RINGING BELL

new material

first finger on A and E strings

Ann and Eg – bert, George as well, are listen – ing to the ring – ing bell; It's

swing – ing, ring – ing, swing – ing, ring – ing mak – ing them sing Ding Dong Bell.

Variations : 1 - 6

8. SAIL IN A PAIL

new material

Dan – iel and Eg – bert have gone for a sail, Float – ing a-

- long in a plas – tic pail; Spin – ning and rock – ing a-

Variation : 8

9. JONATHAN RAT

new material
first finger on D string

Cheerfully

pizzicato

Jon - a - than Rat and Ben - ja - min Cat are try - ing each

oth - er's new coat and hat. No - thing will fit; there's

no help for it, the Rat's too thin, the Cat is too fat!

10. GEORGE GOT OUT OF BED TOO LATE

new material
first finger on G string

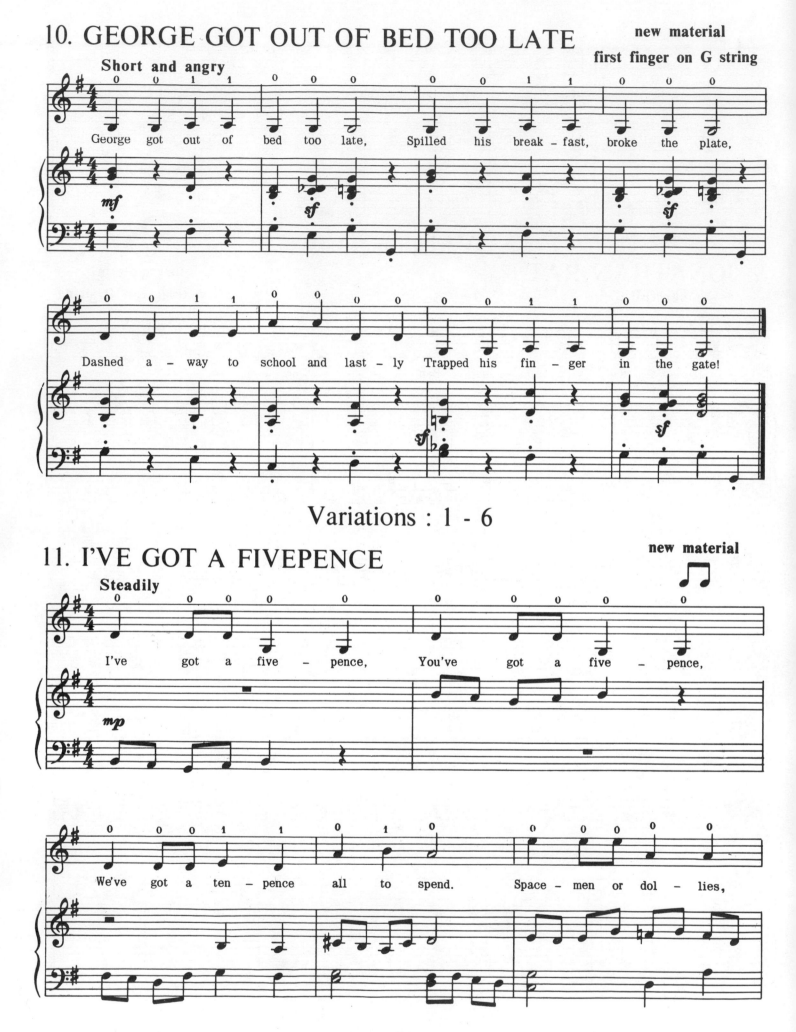

George got out of bed too late, Spilled his break - fast, broke the plate,

Dashed a - way to school and last - ly Trapped his fin - ger in the gate!

Variations : 1 - 6

11. I'VE GOT A FIVEPENCE

new material

I've got a five - pence, You've got a five - pence,

We've got a ten - pence all to spend. Space - men or dol - lies,

12. LULLABY

new material

optional slurs

Choc' late drops or lol – lies, or shall we take a pre – sent home for a friend?

Peacefully

Lul – la – by do not cry, Lul – la, Lul – la Lul – la – by.

Snug and warm, free from harm, Safe from dan – ger and a – larm,

Lul – la – by do not cry, Lul – la, Lul – la, Lul – la – by.

14

13. DON'T BOTHER ME

new material

Angrily

Don't both-er me please can't you see I'm just not free now? Do go a-way,

fuss - ing to - day I can - not al - low. Yes, I can see you're just not free.

you're ne - ver free now! And if I must play without fuss, will you tell me how?

14. RAINY DAY

new material

second finger

Steadily

Dan and Ann went walk - ing, walk - ing, went out walk - ing in the rain;

B.& H.20183

15. THREE IN A BAR

new material

B.& H.20183

16. OVER THE WATER

Smooth and flowing

O – ver the wa – ter we'll be sail – ing, out o – ver the sea. You can be Cap – tain, I shall be more than glad just to be O – ver the wa – ter, sail – ing o – ver the sea.

17. HOLIDAY

new material

compound time

Cheerfully

Hol - i - day time and we're out in the wind, Clam - ber - ing up to the hill tops,

Scrambl - ling, slither - ing, tum - bl - ing down, run - ning a - way for the day.

Chasing and leap - ing or stalk - ing and creep - ing or un - der a ledge while the rain stops:

Hol - i - day time is for games in the wind, ne - ver mind the rain - drops.

18

18. THE CENTIPEDE

Steadily Crawling

new material
third finger, ♪

p, f

B.& H.20183

19. FIDDLER'S FANCY

20. COWBOY TUNE

new material
fourth finger